discovermore

Life in a Community

What Is a Community?

Dwayne Hicks

Britannica Educational Publishing

IN ASSOCIATION WITH

THE ROSEN PUBLISHING GROUP

Published in 2024 by Britannica Educational Publishing (a trademark of Encyclopædia Britannica, Inc.) in association with The Rosen Publishing Group, Inc.
2544 Clinton Street, Buffalo, NY 14224

Distributed exclusively by Rosen Publishing.
To see additional Britannica Educational Publishing titles, go to rosenpublishing.com.

Editor: Kathleen Klatte
Book Design: Leslie Taylor

Photo Credits: Cover Rawpixel.com/Shutterstock.com; (series background) Dai Yim/Shutterstock.com; p. 4 Monkey Business Images/Shutterstock.com; p. 5 Ev. Safronov/Shutterstock.com; p. 6 AshTproductions/Shutterstock.com; p. 7 Brett Taylor Photography/Shutterstock.com; p. 8 mark reinstein/Shutterstock.com; p. 9 LittleRedDragon/Shutterstock.com; p. 11 (top) Romaine W/Shutterstock.com, (bottom) EvgenySHCH/Shutterstock.com; p. 12 Csaba Peterdi/Shutterstock.com; p. 13 Pavel L Photo and Video/Shutterstock.com; p. 14 Lena Platonova/Shutterstock.com; p. 15 Kristi Blokhin/Shutterstock.com; p. 17 (top) Victoria Lipov/Shutterstock.com, (bottom) Jorge Salcedo/Shuttetstock.com; p. 18 Monkey Business Images/Shutterstock.com; p.19 Dmytro Zinkevych/Shutterstock.com; p. 20 Anneka/Shutterstock.com; p. 21 Tyler Olson/Shutterstock.com; p. 22 Monkey Business Images/Shutterstock.com; p. 23 wavebreakmedia/Shutterstock.com; p. 25 (top) Monkey Business Images/Shutterstock.com, (bottom) Ground Picture/Shutterstock.com; p. 27 (top) VGstockstudio/Shutterstock.com, (bottom) Cheryl Casey/Shutterstock.com; p. 29 (top) Nicole Glass Photography/Shutterstock.com, (bottom) Iurii Osadchi/Shutterstock.com.

Cataloging-in-Publication Data

Names: Hicks, Dwayne.
Title: What is a community? / Dwayne Hicks.
Description: New York : Britannica Educational Publishing, in Association with Rosen Educational Services. 2024. | Series: Discover more: life in a community | Includes glossary and index.
Identifiers: ISBN 9781642828900 (library bound) | ISBN 9781642828894 (pbk) | ISBN 9781642828917 (ebook)
Subjects: LCSH: Communities--Juvenile literature. | Community life--Juvenile literature. | Community development--Juvenile literature.
Classification: LCC HM756.H53 2024 | DDC 307–dc23

Manufactured in the United States of America

CPSIA Compliance Information: Batch #CSBRIT24. For further information contact Rosen Publishing at 1-800-237-9932.

Contents

Coming Together

A community is a group of people who come together for the common good. Each community is unique. Yet they all have things in common. A community can be a group of people living in a particular area. A community can also be a group of people with common interests who may or may not live together.

A community can be made up of a large or small group of people. The land area of a community can also be large or small. A community may be roomy or crowded, depending on the size of its land area and how many people live there.

Your neighborhood is a physical community. Neighbors live close together.

Members of online communities share common interests, like gaming. They may or may not live nearby or know one another in real life.

Every community has **boundaries**. Boundaries can involve the actual space a community has or uses. Rules about membership or behavior within the community might also create boundaries. How many different communities do you belong to?

WORD WISE

A boundary is a physical marker, like a fence or river, that shows where one area ends and another begins. It can also mean the limits of acceptable behavior.

All Together Now!

Communities form because people are social and usually work better as a group. Community members often band together to reach goals or to get things they need or want. The things they need can include goods and services. Goods are items that people use, and services are things people do for others.

However, being in a community is not just about getting something. Members also have to give back to make sure that a community is successful.

If everyone puts their own garbage in the trash can, no one has to look at an ugly mess and no one person has to spend a lot of time picking up after everyone else.

People shovel the sidewalk in winter so others can walk safely and mail can be delivered.

Each person has a role to play. Some people may be leaders who organize community activities. Others show their support by sharing their time, talent, or treasure (money or goods). They might volunteer their time to clean up their neighborhood or they might teach others a new skill. Communities work best when everyone cooperates and follows the rules.

Consider This

A social contract is the idea that people give up small amounts of personal freedom to make their community work better. For example, during the COVID-19 pandemic, people wore masks in public to slow the spread of the disease.

What Makes a Community Work Well?

You may have noticed that some communities work better than others. Their members are happy and they work well together. People have studied different communities to find out why this happens. They have found that most successful communities have four things in common.

A public hearing is a meeting where people can learn about proposed changes to their community.

Some people might like the idea of a fast food restaurant near their neighborhood. Others might worry about things like traffic or trash.

Members of successful communities feel as if they belong and have things in common with others in their community. Community members should also feel as if they have influence in the group. They want to be able to make a difference, both through and within the group. Happy communities have members who bring different skills and views to the community.

Finally, members of a community should share history, experiences, and time together. These connections create important bonds. People work better together when they trust each other and know that everyone is dedicated to making the community successful.

Consider This

Have you ever worked on a group project for school? It works best when everyone does their part, doesn't it?

Places Where People Live

One of the most common types of communities is the geographic community. This kind of community is formed by many people living in the same area.

Geography is a science that deals with Earth's surface. Physical geography describes the land and its features, like mountains, lakes, and deserts. They affect how each community is built and survives. Human geography describes how groups of people live within geographic areas. Human geographers might study why communities develop in certain places. Others study a community's culture, including customs, languages, and religions.

Geographic communities are defined by physical boundaries, as well as how the people within them live. Neighborhoods, cities, states, and nations are all geographic communities.

Tuvalu is an island nation in the Pacific Ocean.

compare and contrast

Imagine you lived in an island community where most supplies had to be imported. How would your life be different? How would it be the same?

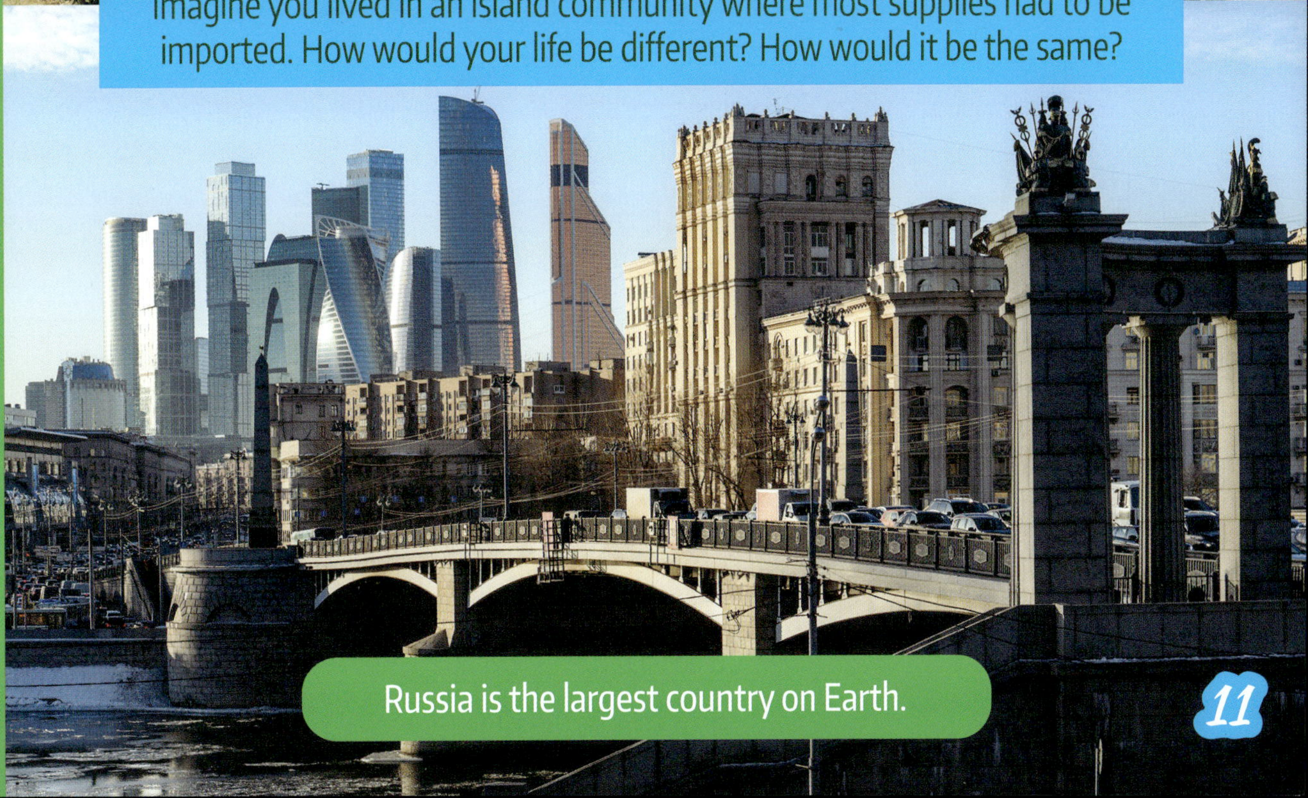

Russia is the largest country on Earth.

Urban Communities

Urban communities, called cities, are places where many people live and work close together. However, geography is not the only thing shared by these communities. People who live and work in cities share resources and services, and everyone must also obey the city's laws.

There is often a pattern to how cities are built. In the middle of the city is usually an area called downtown. This area has office buildings and big stores. Cities also may have one or more areas of factories and storage buildings outside of the downtown area.

Many of the oldest cities in the world grew up along rivers. The river Thames flows through London.

The Smithsonian Institution is a group of important American museums. Many are located in Washington, D.C. People travel from all over the world to visit them.

Cities also have houses and apartment buildings, where people live. Throughout the city are places where people can relax and have fun. Most cities have restaurants and parks. Large cities might have theaters and museums.

Consider This

A large city might have a lot of rules about things like where people can park their cars. Why do you think that is?

Suburban Communities

Smaller communities, called suburbs, as located near cities. They can be towns, villages, or small cities.

Towns are considered local communities, meaning community members live and work closely together within a small, set space. They share local services and facilities. Smaller than cities, towns tend to have more houses and apartments than businesses.

Suburban communities tend to be **residential** instead of commercial.

In a rural community, people might have to drive several miles into town to go shopping or get their hair cut.

Villages are even smaller than towns. Towns and villages have their own shopping and businesses, but some people who live in suburbs commute, or travel, to jobs in the city.

Beyond the suburbs are rural communities. A rural community is sometimes called the country or the countryside. It has fewer people living in a much larger area, so its homes and buildings are spread far apart. Rural communities often include farms or ranches.

WORD WISE

A residential area is intended for people to live in. Many people raise families in residential areas.

Your Neighbors

Your neighbors are the people who live closest to you. Often people like to live near people they have things in common with. They form small communities called neighborhoods.

Neighborhoods are located within cities, towns, and villages. Town neighborhoods are located on a street or two. Neighborhoods in big cities may be spread across several blocks or even a few miles.

Sometimes neighborhoods are known for a geographical feature such as a lake or a hill. Many large cities, such as New York and Los Angeles, have ethnic neighborhoods. These neighborhoods have many people from one particular culture living and working in them.

Often, people choose a neighborhood based on how much money they make or the kind of work they do.

Little Italy is a neighborhood in New York City. A long time ago, many Italian immigrants settled there when they arrived in America.

compare and contrast

In a city neighborhood, you might be able to walk from your apartment to a bodega or small restaurant. Do you think that's possible in a suburban neighborhood? Or a rural one?

Beacon Hill is a historic neighborhood in Boston, Massachusetts. It got its name because the original settlers built a beacon on top of a hill to warn nearby communities of danger.

Where the Community Comes Together

Every community needs a place where residents can come together. Often, that place is a community center. The main purpose of a community center is to develop and improve a neighborhood.

The first community center was founded in 1884. It was called Toynbee Hall and was located in a poor area of London, England. University students worked with community members to improve the living conditions of their neighborhood.

Some community centers offer fun activities for elderly people. Being able to get out of their homes and do things with other people helps keep them mentally alert.

A community center might also provide for basic needs, such as hot meals.

The first community center in the United States opened in New York City in 1886. Others soon followed in cities such as Chicago and Boston.

Today's community centers provide services meant to improve living conditions for members of the surrounding community. They offer classes and activities for adults and children. These activities include things like music and sports.

Community centers may also offer other services for the people of a neighborhood. They might include things like health screenings, afterschool activities, and tax preparation.

Consider This

Community centers often offer programs for free or minimal cost. How does this help the community?

What Makes Us Who We Are

Everyone has a set of features that makes them who they are. These features add up to a person's identity. These features include age and **gender**. How and where someone is raised, the kind of schooling they receive, and other life experiences also can affect identity. Some communities are made up of people who share some of those features.

Catholic nuns have several communities in common. They identify as female and they share the same beliefs. These are communities of identity. They may also share a physical community, such as a convent.

Firefighters belong to community of identity. They share a profession. They've also gone through the same type of training and share many personality traits.

A community of identity brings together people who share one or more qualities or experiences. For instance, people are part of a community based on their gender or gender identity. They may share experiences and feel part of a community with other people who identify as their same gender.

Culture also affects identity. Culture is a pattern of behavior shared by a group of people. It involves shared food, language, clothing, music, customs, beliefs, and religion. People from the same culture may share a community of culture, as well as a physical community.

WORD WISE

Gender is a person's own sense of being male, female, some combination of male and female, or neither male nor female.

The Family Unit

One of the most basic types of community is the family. It is the first kind that most people experience. A family is two or more people connected by biology, adoption, marriage, or strong emotions. A family can be considered a type of community of identity because people's identities are shaped, in part, by their families.

Members of a family are part of a community based on their relationships with each other. Families regularly share resources, such as food, water, and electricity. Family members often combine their money in order to be able to afford these types of resources.

Families can be formed by adoption, not just biology.

When families work together on volunteer projects in their community, both groups are strengthened.

Family members also regularly interact with one another—hopefully in mainly good ways. Family members should always be able to count on one another for love and encouragement.

Consider This

The term "found family" refers to a group of individuals who choose to form a family unit to support and care for one another, even though they're not related by blood or marriage.

What Do We Have In Common?

People who share a common interest or hobby often form communities. In this type of community, members do not need to live close to each other.

People share many different kinds of interests. Some young people enjoy scouting. Adults who were part of a scouting troop when they were younger may choose to continue to be a part of that community by being a scout leader. Playing in the school band shows community spirit through music. People who collect and swap trading cards belong to a community that is interested in a particular type of card game. People who enjoy a certain sport and play it or travel to watch professional games are part of a community, too.

A book club is a group of people who read the same book, then share their thoughts about it. Libraries and bookstores often host book clubs.

compareandcontrast

Many communities are online today. People who enjoy a certain computer game can play with others who enjoy it, no matter where they live. How do you think this differs from games played by a group in the same room?

Members of the armed forces are part of the military community. After their service, they may choose to be part of a community of veterans.

At School

Schools can be part of many types of communities, all at the same time. They can be considered geographic communities because students often go to schools in or near their neighborhood.

Schools run by religious organizations could be thought of as communities of identity. The teachers and the students share certain beliefs that define who they are. All-boy and all-girl schools can also be communities of identity.

Finally, schools can be called communities of interest. For example, students with an interest in, or talent for, music or theater might choose to attend a school for the arts. All schools share the idea that learning—whether it's facts, sports, or an art—is good for the community.

Students at a professional ballet school are part of several communities. Can you name some?

compare and contrast

How do you think a dance school or art school is different from regular school? How is it the same?

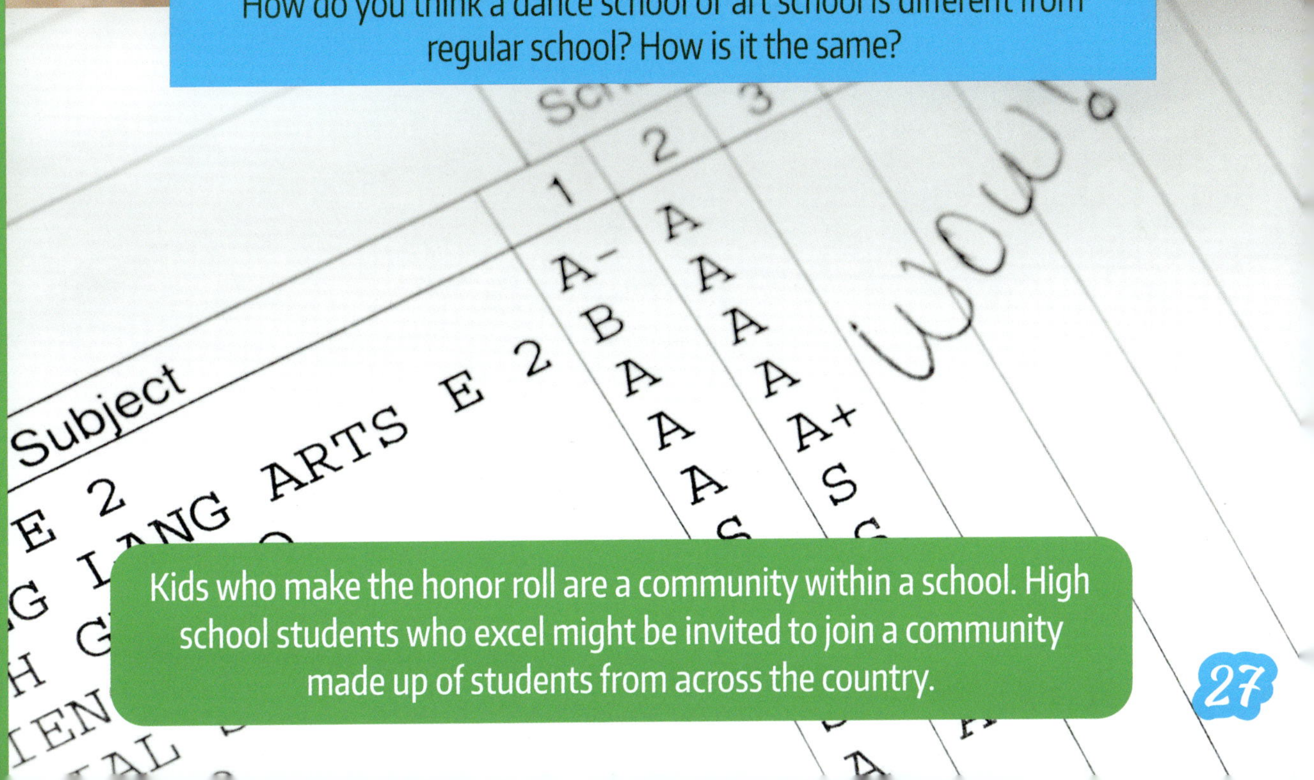

Kids who make the honor roll are a community within a school. High school students who excel might be invited to join a community made up of students from across the country.

The Biggest Community of All

There's one community that's bigger than all the others. We all belong to it. Can you guess what it is?

Each geographic community can be part of a bigger community. For example, a neighborhood is part of a city. Cities, suburbs, and urban areas are also part of larger areas called states or provinces. Those states and provinces are parts of countries. Countries around the world are part of the global community. They work together through organizations such the United Nations. They also sell goods to one another.

Because we all share the planet, individual people all over the world are also members of the global community. If we all work together, we can make our global community a good place for all the people who live here, as well as the earth itself.

Environmental activists are a community of like-minded individuals committed to protecting the earth for our global community.

compareandcontrast

Check out the labels on products around your home. How many were made in other countries? Why do you suppose that item was imported, rather than made locally?

The Olympic Games are a global celebration of excellence in sport. Many athletes come together from around the world with shared interests, talents, and goals.

Glossary

band: To gather together.

boundary: A dividing line; something that shows a limit or end.

commercial: Related to or used in the buying and selling of goods and services.

culture: A pattern of behavior shared by a group of people.

ethnic: Of or relating to groups of people with common traits and customs and a sense of shared identity.

geographic: Having to do with the natural features of a place.

global: Involving the entire world.

goods: Objects or products that people can buy and use.

identity: The qualities that make a particular person or group different from others.

import: To bring a product into a country to be sold.

interact: Talking or doing something with other people.

professional: Paid to participate in a sport or activity.

resource: Something that can be used by people.

services: Things that people do for others.

urban: Of or relating to cities.

For More Information

Books

Kalman, Bobbie. *Community Helpers*. New York, NY: Lightbox Learning, 2023.

Rustad, Martha E. H. *How Can People Help Communities?* North Mankato, MN: Capstone Editions, 2020.

Websites

Helping Others
sesameworkshop.org/resources/helping-others
Enjoy this short video about helping others by the Sesame Street team.

Youth Service America
ysa.org
Youth Service America is a site that helps young people find opportunities to volunteer and be of service in their community.

Index